The MAGIC *of Believing*

Believe In Yourself And The Universe Is Forced To Believe In You

⊱•⊰

Vic Johnson

Published by:
Laurenzana Press
PO Box 1220
Melrose, FL 32666 USA

www.LaurenzanaPress.com
****

ISBN-13: 978-1-937918-63-7

CONTENTS

introduction

The Size of Your Success Is Determined by The Size of Your Belief

"***The size of your success is determined by the size of your belief.*** " Those thirteen simple words rocked my life on a Saturday night in October 1997.

I was attending a seminar in Jacksonville, Florida, when the speaker uttered those words. As I look back on it now, it's amazing that I had read them several times before that night in the classic book, *The Magic of Thinking Big,* by Dr. David Schwartz.

The impact they had was almost mystical. Something in my Spirit erupted upon hearing those words, and I knew instantly that I'd been given the answer I'd been seeking for the better part of five years (but really for my entire life).

Before that night: Eighteen months before that

Saturday night, my family and I were unceremoniously evicted from our home. We'd been given 48 hours by a judge to find a new place to live, although we had no money and nowhere to go.

Five months earlier our car had been repossessed (I drove to the event in a 12-year-old bomb I borrowed from a friend). We qualified below the U.S. poverty level for a family of five, and I earned just $14,027 for the entire year.

After that night: Within 90 days of that night, big things began to happen. People and opportunities seemed to come out of the woodwork (they had been there all along, but I couldn't see them because of my lack of belief). Within one year I was earning a six-figure income. Within five years I was earning as much in one week as I had earned the entire year of 1997. And within ten years I was earning TEN TIMES THAT IN JUST ONE DAY!

I'm not giving you the before-and-after scenario as a means of bragging, as I'm very humbled by what happened. I'm sharing it with you to emphasize this isn't some get rich theory I read in a pie-in-the-sky book. This is what I've used – and what I've taught thousands of others to use – that took me from a miserable, godforsaken experience to a seven-figure income, a celebrity in the personal development industry, and the chance to live the dreams I previously could only imagine.

It's my opinion that **belief** is a key element that can

mean the difference between achievement and failure. Now, some people would argue that persistence is the key element, but I would respond that you can't persist if you don't have belief. Other people would argue that preparation is the most important element. While I would agree that being prepared is important, being prepared won't matter if you don't have the belief that you will succeed.

As James Allen author of the classic *As A Man Thinketh* wrote, "Belief precedes all action."

In the early 1950s, a runner named Roger Bannister discovered the power of that statement. Bannister was by no means a picture of failure. In fact, he was an Olympic runner, having set a British record of 3:46.30 in the men's 1,500-meter event at the Summer Olympics in Helsinki, Finland.

The British record was a success, but it wasn't enough for Bannister who had placed fourth in that event, just missing out on a bronze medal. It wasn't enough to make him feel happy about what he'd accomplished.

So after a few months of deciding whether or not he wanted to continue being a runner, Bannister made a decision that would change his life. He decided to place his belief in himself *before* the accomplishment came. That he would believe *first*, then watch that belief play out in real life.

In this case, the belief seemed like a far-fetched

notion, because he believed it was possible that a mile could be run in under four minutes.

At first there wasn't much to support his theory. If it hadn't been done in the previous 6,000+ years of human existence, what would make him think he could achieve it? Sure, he could run a mile in just over four minutes, and was one of the fastest human beings alive. But other runners like John Landy, who was perhaps faster than Bannister, couldn't hit under the four-minute mark even in peak condition.

But Bannister was invigorated by his new self-imposed challenge. As a medical student, he was very familiar with human anatomy. He knew that for centuries the medical community had dismissed the notion of such a feat, saying that a human heart could never survive the experience.

His answer was to create an experiment in physiology. *There is a heart, there are muscles, there are lungs,* he thought. He then asked, "To what extent can this piece of human machinery be trained to do a very specific, very skilled task?" His answer was what created his belief that his goal was possible.

In 1953, Bannister broke the British mile record by getting his time down to only 3.5 seconds over four minutes. He later said it was this race that convinced him the four-minute mile was not out of reach. Meanwhile, other runners like Landy and Wes Santee made attempts at beating Bannister's time, but were still over the four-minute mile.

The next summer in 1954, Bannister knew that Landy was hot on his heels, and it was time to make his attempt at the seemingly impossible. He did so at a race in Oxford, England, finishing at a total of 3:59.4 – six-tenths of a second under four minutes! And as they say, the rest of the story is history.

Then other competitive runners all over the world followed suit, and were soon breaking the four-minute mile barrier. What had been previously impossible was becoming simply a matter of routine. Let me repeat that: *Simply a matter of routine.* It's a stunning fact. Human beings have to run 15 miles per hour sustained for under four minutes to run a mile that fast. And now it was something runners worldwide could accomplish because Bannister proved running a four-minute mile to be true.

Yet, the real problem was never about human anatomy. Roger Bannister, John Landy and others had it in them to run the four-minute mile all along, and proved their bodies weren't different from their ancestors. All along human beings had possessed the gift of running a mile in under four minutes.

So what was the difference? They **believed** they could do it, plain and simple.

Roger Bannister's belief in his ability to run an under four-minute mile before he actually accomplished it became the foundation for his spectacular achievement.

Then when others saw it was possible, their successes followed behind him.

You see, it's *belief* that makes the difference (not *circumstances* or *limitations* which are by-products of a person's beliefs). Having faith not only in yourself but in the accomplishments you could achieve is a simple but powerful concept.

First, belief requires that you *visualize* yourself achieving something even before it is achieved.

Second, belief creates the positive reinforcement cycle that keeps you motivated even beyond failure. After all, who would want to give up if they truly believed that success was just around the corner? What they *know* to be true is how they keep themselves moving. *Success is just around the corner,* they think, and so it becomes a reality.

The core trait of *persistence* is belief. If you didn't have the belief that you would succeed at some point, you'd have nothing to justify your decision to hang in there. And hanging in there is the bridge that sets the super successful apart from everyone else.

Napoleon Hill, author of the classic book *Think and Grow Rich*, interviewed over 500 of the most successful people in the world at that time. He said that persistence was the only common trait he identified in all of them.

Having belief alone may not be enough to accomplish much of anything. Action and desire also play heavily into the success formula. But when you start to see the role belief has in shaping the very circumstances around you, you'll begin to see just how *powerful* it can be.

You see, faith and belief are strongly tied into just about every element of motivation. When you have a weak belief, it's hard to motivate yourself to take action. *What's the use,* you wonder, *when I know I'm not going to achieve anything?*

When you have a weak belief, your desire to achieve will lag behind. "I'm not sure I even want this goal," you say. "Maybe I'm supposed to be doing something else."

Are those the thoughts of someone who's so super-charged with faith and belief that their ultimate success is a matter of *destiny*? Of course not! Similarly, it will be hard to achieve any great feat in your life without first believing you can do it.

But the role of believing in your life is more comprehensive than that. In *As a Man Thinketh* Allen notes that just about all surroundings are the result of faith and belief. What people *expect* is ultimately what they get.

If you're willing to accept that fact, then only one question remains: How can belief be changed? After all, strong beliefs aren't forged overnight. Perhaps not, but you can start changing them *now*. This is important to remember, because your beliefs help regulate your internal thermostat which reflects your deeply embedded standards.

If you're comfortable earning only $20,000 a year,

being 20 pounds overweight, or not being your own boss, it's because you have become comfortable and set in your ways. Adjusting that internal thermostat is how you put yourself on a similar level of thinking *of belief* as those who are already successful.

I have a quote taped to my computer by Orison Swett Marden: "*We lift ourselves by our thought. We climb upon our vision of ourselves. If you want to enlarge your life, you must first enlarge your thought of it and of yourself. Hold the ideal of yourself as you long to be, always everywhere.*" Now that's how to go about adjusting your internal thermostat!

In this book I'll detail the exact roles belief plays in your daily life, and what you can do to change the results you've been trying to get in your efforts for attaining success.

If you want to turn up that thermostat and your beliefs to change the world around you, it's time to read on.

So let's get started!

Attention All Eagle Eyes: We've had a number of people proof this book before we released it to you, but there is a chance you might spot something that was missed. If you find a typo or other obvious error please send it to us. And if you're the first one to report it, we'll send you a free gift! Send to: corrections@laurenzanapress.com

1

What is Belief? And What is Faith?

To have an idea of what true faith and belief look like, let's take a look at the *results* they create and how they motivate you.

Consider the true story of Maxcy Filer that Cynthia Kersey wrote about in her incredible book, *Unstoppable* (which I strongly URGE you to add to your library). In 1966, Maxcy knew he wanted to be a lawyer. So that year he took the bar exam in California ... and failed. But that's not particularly unique, because failing the bar happens to most novice lawyers across the country on a regular basis.

However, Maxcy Filer's story isn't one about failure. He took the bar exam again and failed. Then he took it again and failed again. Then he took it once again and he failed once again.

Is this a story of persistence and short-term failure? Not even close! Filer *kept* taking the exam and *kept* failing. He took the bar everywhere it was offered in California: Los Angeles, San Diego, Riverside and San Francisco, thinking that maybe the location of the test would affect the results. But Maxcy Filer failed, failed, failed, failed……..

He tried for so long and failed so many times that his sons grew up, went to law school, took the bar, and passed it before he did. But ever persistent, Maxcy took the bar exam again. And guess what happened? Success? The triumph of his will over the circumstances, or sheer willpower over his talent and preparation? Nope! As you can guess, he failed again.

One of Maxcy's sons went to work as a lawyer and hired his father to be a law clerk. In that legal setting you'd think Filer would have an advantage in learning exactly what he needed to do to pass that bar exam. So he took it again. And he failed again.

Then at 61 years old, Maxcy took the bar exam again. Having spent *tens of thousands of dollars* on fees, countless hours studying – not to mention the decades spent failing and watching his children grow up and pass the exam – Maxcy Filer finally – *finally!* – passed the bar on his 48th attempt.

So what does this story say about belief? Maybe it's

more an example of extreme persistence in the face of failure – about using pure will and a desire to continue on.

Think about where Maxcy might have ended up if he didn't have the belief that the next time he took the bar he *might* succeed. But just the sheer belief that he *might* succeed was enough to keep him trying 48 times over a span of several decades.

His oldest son was in the third grade when he took the test for the first time, and was an established lawyer in his own practice by the time Maxcy became an attorney. It took 25 years and 47 tries from 1966 to 1991 to pass the exam. "Perseverance, perseverance, perseverance," said Filer. "I was going to take it until the last inch of my breath."

Is doing something over and over and expecting a different result the definition of insanity? Most people likely would have quit after a few tries. Maybe a half-dozen, dozen, or two dozen times at the very most. They might have an immense desire to pass. They might take action by studying hard to overcome any perceived deficit in talent.

But what kind of *belief* is necessary to continually put yourself through that kind of failure over and over for half a lifetime (think about the amount of disappointment Maxcy must have felt after failing the exam each time)?

Not to mention the scathing remarks he probably heard from family, friends and colleagues after all his unsuccessful attempts. You know what I'm talking about. Those "well-meaning" souls who are supposedly thinking of your best interests while hinting you're not cut out for that job or profession you've always wanted.

Maxcy probably had negative people like that in his life. But he had a louder voice inside – the voice of his belief – that ***drowned out the voices of all the naysayers.***

Sure, *desire* helps in cases like this. But no matter how much you desire something, you're not going to work for it if you truly believe you can't get it. What would be the point? But just believing in the *chance* you could succeed can be enough of a spark to motivate you to greater action.

That's what rock-solid belief looks like in the real world.

So What Exactly is Belief? And Why Does it Matter?

When combined, the components of belief, desire, and action create a unique, character-defining quality. Belief is the seed the tree sprouted from. Desire and action are two of many branches that lead to persistence, passion, and purpose (the leaves).

For our purposes here, the definition of a belief is ***a perception, an assertion, or an attitude that is held***

in strong conviction. Although it's a rather innocuous, scientific way of defining belief, each component has a perfect meaning of truth you can apply to your life.

Beliefs stand alone in their existence. They can be an assertion such as "I believe I'll be late to work today." Or "I believe I'm a capable person." They can even be perceptions like "Judy doesn't like me." (Yes, perceptions can be a belief as they're subjective observations of a person, situation or event. A perception becomes a person's belief because it rings true for them.)

To that end, a belief is something you hold to be true. But a belief that becomes an assumption can lead to skewed perceptions, mistakes, bad judgments and decisions (many of these mistaken beliefs will be addressed further on). Your beliefs can make you **perceive two different things about the same experience.**

In her book, *Choose the Happiness Habit,* Pam Golden wrote about twin brothers who had identical experiences as children (as is common with twins). But one became a mega-successful multi-millionaire, while the other became literally a skid-row bum.

During her interviews with the men, Golden determined it was their inner belief about those experiences that had altered their perceptions. When she asked each twin what they thought led to their success and failure, they individually said it was because their parents were alcoholics.

One rose out of the ashes of his childhood trauma

to become empowered and successful. The other became embittered and victimized. It was their *belief* about the experience with their parents and not the experience itself that defined their ultimate ability to achieve (or not achieve) success in life.

Golden's research validated the existence of subjective reality, since both boys experienced the same suffering that determined how they would become as men. It also revealed how the power of perception can ultimately change the way the world is navigated.

That's what belief is and why it matters.

Is Faith the Same as Belief?

I always say that faith and belief are "first cousins." In order to understand the subtle difference between the two – and since belief was previously discussed – it's important to try to define what faith is.

Paul, the apostle, provided a brilliant definition of faith in the Hebrews 11:1 when he wrote, "Now faith is the substance of things hoped for, the evidence of things not seen."

I feel he was saying that belief is the conviction people hold, and faith is the confidence the belief will be realized. So collectively, faith and belief become the most powerful force on earth.

In James 2:14-26, it is written that "faith without works is dead." In other words, if you fail to take action on a belief, then your faith in that belief will wither and die. Which is why it's possible to have weak faith while strongly believing in something.

"Well, if faith is so powerful," you might say, "then it should work no matter where I am. I could be lying on the couch watching TV, or running a marathon, and faith is doing its job."

People don't tend to realize that *action* and *inaction* are both forms of thought. By staying on the couch they're accepting that there's nothing better in the universe than the couch.

But if they had faith there was a great opportunity waiting for them – such as winning a marathon – would they really sit on the couch all day? Absolutely not! They'd get up and run their way to success. Being inactive on a couch all day means their faith is probably weak; running in a marathon means their faith is strong (inaction vs. action). Therefore, their expectation becomes their reality.

But there's another quality to faith I'd like to address, which is its power to overcome obstacles. When people are facing struggles, they often forget that others are experiencing similar or bigger problems.

For example, let's say you suffer from ADD, which can be quite a mental hurdle to overcome. *Forbes* magazine did a survey of the top 500 CEOs in America, and found that 30% suffer from an attention deficit disorder. Did they have a magical form of ADD that didn't affect their lives? Or did they find ways to beat their obstacles through faith and persistence?

Having *faith* is all about taking action and maintaining a positive belief in spite of obstacles and self-sabotaging arguments. Faith keeps you going when you want to start a business and your "well meaning" friends say, "It's a tough economy. You'll be lucky to succeed after a year!" Or "There's no room for another restaurant [or hot dog stand or balloon bouquet salesman]. Why would you want to do this in such a tough market?" Naysayers project their *lack of faith* on you because of what they would/wouldn't do themselves.

There's no such thing as "blind" faith, because faith means you have the foresight of the end result before it occurs. While other people focus on the negatives and obstacles, you will stay focused on the end result and your ultimate goal. Having faith means allowing your balloon to rise to great heights, instead of allowing others to let the air out of your balloon.

Faith not only feeds perception, it is also fed by perception. When you have faith in an end result, your perceptions change to support that belief. When someone tells you about why an economic downturn is a bad time to start a business, positive thinking would be "I'd hate to start a business when everyone else is starting one too. I'd rather start a business when there's little competition." The same situation with two different beliefs, two different perceptions, but with your own faith in your desire to succeed.

Hopefully you're starting to see how belief and faith can alter your perceptions. These two driving forces behind success are so potent that they can literally change your life.

2

Overcoming Your Belief in Helplessness

Belief is simply what a person accepts as true or real. (Note that I didn't say your belief is about what is true or real; it's simply what you accept as true or real.) So what does this have to do with overcoming helplessness?

It's a fact that human beings are capable of great achievements. But consider for a moment how people have conquered their limitations and turned them into opportunities:

- **Age:** By the time Harland David "Colonel" Sanders turned 65, he had only owned one small chicken restaurant before turning his Kentucky Fried chicken recipe into a multi-million dollar franchise.

- **Speed:** Remember Roger Bannister mentioned earlier?

- **Means:** Andrew Carnegie started out at $2.50 per week as a telegraph messenger boy, and ended up donating millions of dollars in philanthropic efforts during his lifetime.

- **Physical Incapacitation:** Although Nick Vujicic was born without arms and legs (tetra-amelia syndrome), he rose above his limitations to become a world-renowned motivational speaker. Nick is married, runs a non-profit organization called "Life Without Limbs," and writes books. He says his faith is big enough to overcome any and all disabilities. So if you have all four limbs and can climb any mountain, where does your lack of faith and helplessness stem from?

- **College Degree:** Bill Gates didn't have a college degree when he brought Microsoft to the forefront of the business world. Of course degrees help during your climb up the success ladder, but a lack of one should not be an obstacle to achieving your goals. A degree is a tool; you are the talent and the intelligence.

- **Intelligence:** I don't want to call anyone dumb. So let me just say that I can name plenty of high-achievers who aren't intelligent, but have managed to become very successful and wealthy.

I'd like to think that these examples have ignited your faith a little bit. But to achieve positive, permanent changes in your life, you're going to have to change the way you perceive your life.

Because your way of thinking is more of a habit than a singular thought, change can be difficult. And like most habits, your belief in yourself will have profound effects on your life because it affects what you do on a daily basis.

Overcoming the belief of helplessness – those limiting thoughts that can hold you back – is a vitally important step to substituting sabotaging beliefs with a more constructive way of viewing the world.

What Comes First, the Belief or the Reality?

Take a hard look at who you are today and your circumstances at this very moment. What – or who – do you think created those circumstances in the first place?

You did, of course.

Your current situation is a result of the actions, beliefs, and desires you've had in the past. If you can accept this fact and let go of previous disappointments, you can change the present and your future. (This can be a hard concept to swallow, particularly when your current outlook isn't too sunny. But hang in there with me.)

Even if you weren't as proactive about your choices as you could have been in the past, you can't immediately skyrocket to your new life in the future. Your belief in you doesn't begin once you've foreseen a bright and positive outcome. You and only you have the power to create a new life, and it all starts by shifting your beliefs.

The first step is **accepting that you created your own circumstances**. Even if it doesn't paint a very flattering portrayal of who you've been up to this point, it's imperative to do this to move your life forward.

If you're close to hitting rock bottom, acknowledging your role in getting there can be a life-altering experience. Even if you're not happy in your current situation, you can feel the immense power that comes with accepting responsibility for your choices. Belief is a choice. Faith is a choice. Combining them to pull yourself up by the boot straps and living the life you deserve is a choice.

Accepting my role in creating my circumstances was simultaneously one of the lowest and most powerful days I've ever experienced.

My family and I had been given a notice of eviction, which was followed by the repossession of our car. The utilities had been turned off because I couldn't pay the bill. I was so broke that I couldn't even buy my daughter a birthday present on the day she became a teenager.

And there in all that turmoil I'm reading in Emmet Fox's *Make Your Life Worthwhile* that I had created everything. I alone was solely responsible for my family's demise. Can you imagine how sick that made me feel? I couldn't begin to imagine how I created such ugliness and pain. In my denial I blamed the economy, my spouse, getting screwed in a business deal, bad luck and sun flares. The way I was feeling it could have been a nun in St. Peter's Church. It had to be something else but me that brought down the roof around my family.

But as I kept reading and re-reading Fox's book, the realization of my responsibility became clearer and more profound. And I felt something very powerful welling up inside of me.

Then in a flash, the biggest epiphany I'd ever had in my life loomed in front of me: If I was 100% responsible for creating my mess, I could also create a way out. I knew in that instant that if you can steer left toward disaster, you can steer right toward success. And I was the only one who could keep me from achieving success. It was that simple.

Of course it doesn't always seem that simple when your *perceived* reality looks permanent and inflexible. Although your problems can feel at times like sidewalk concrete, your individual situation can be poured into a new, more malleable form. You can alter a severely negative perception by changing it to a very positive focus.

At this point ask yourself if your circumstances are tangible. Can you see, hear and touch them? Do you have evidence that they exist? For example, a text message may say your partner wants to see other people. But it's the *meaning* you choose to ascribe to that message that creates a terrible *circumstance.* Maybe they feel you're too good for them, so by projecting their issues into the reality of the situation makes it worse than it needs to be (until you either get to the bottom of things, or realize it's for the best and walk away).

And like me, your perceptions can change your reality in an instant. For instance, if you live in the United States and are living paycheck-to-paycheck, you might feel as poor as dirt. But around you are a plethora of grocery and department stores, restaurants, hairdressers, and service stations catering to your every need.

Even though you may not be able to afford luxuries, can you pay your bills every month? Can you go out to dinner or to a movie? Do you turn on the faucet and drink clean, clear water any time you want? Congratulations, because there are millions of people in the world who consider that a life-saving luxury.

You're probably reading this on an electronic device – a luxury most people can't afford. Do you see it as an enriching part of your life, or something you take for granted? Now that you've given this some thought, are you really poor? Or do you just *believe* you're poor?

How can you change that word "poor" into a different *perception* of your circumstances which might be "limited", "challenged" or that you're smart about how you spend your money on a tight budget? You've just gone from a negative assumption to a positive belief.

If I want to be rich, you might think, *I need to brainwash myself into believing I'm already rich.*

Brainwashing is not belief or faith, and that's not what I'm suggesting at all. But it is important to remember all the good things you've created from your beliefs. Why? Because then you'll have evidence that you are capable of success.

Whatever you want to be needs to be visualized before you can become it. Belief leads to reality which leads to success.

Overcoming Limiting Beliefs

Once you've accepted responsibility for your current circumstances, you're ready for the next step which is getting rid of your limiting beliefs.

Why is this step so important? Clearly you're experiencing some sort of frustration, or you wouldn't be reading my book. Although your life seems good on many levels, you might have some goals you have yet to achieve.

Consider this metaphor: Let's say you've longed for beautiful landscaping around your house. You want flowers planted along the walkway, new trees, and a perfectly groomed lawn to greet the passersby.

You stand outside your house and realize your lawn is full of weeds, overgrown grass, and patches of unplanted dirt. Do you start planting flowers right away? Of course you could, but you wouldn't be addressing the underlying problems with the lawn. You'd just have flowers trying to poke their heads through the tall grass. People walking by would see you as an unsuccessful gardener with a brown thumb.

Instead, you first need to pull the weeds, seed the dirt, plant seedlings and bulbs, and start watering so they can grow into a victory garden. Similarly, you should start your journey to success by removing the limited beliefs that have held you back from growing into the life you've dreamt about having.

What's that you say? You don't think you have any limiting beliefs? Well, my friend, if you assess the reality of your situation you'd probably be quite surprised. So let's look at a few examples of limiting beliefs that can become small or large depending on your perceptions:

- **"I don't have a college degree"**: For years, not having a degree was a limiting belief that messed with my head. I felt uneducated and unemployable, which in turn made me feel less of a provider for my family. You might not feel you deserve to apply to well-paying jobs, and will settle for lesser positions because you think that's where you belong. **Don't believe it for one second**! (Bill Gates and Sir

Richard Branson are two examples of succ
people who didn't have degrees.) Don't let no
having a degree hold you back. There are other
ways to utilize your talents, creativity, skills and intelligence (a trade school where you can hone your skills might be a better choice instead of college). As they say, "There's a lid for every pot." You just have to find the one that fits you!

- **"I like to sleep late in the morning"**: For a long time this was another belief that kept me bogged down. People were telling me "the early bird gets the worm," but I was sick of eating nothing but worms! Successful people swear that waking up at the crack of dawn gets them ahead of their day. But Albert Einstein was a night owl. And when I found out my hero Winston Churchill was a late riser, I let go of my limiting belief and you can as well.

- **"I need to be more organized to be successful"**: My desk and work area never has been the neatest place but success doesn't equate to the condition of your desk (though, granted, an organized desk could probably boost your productivity in a big way). Responding to a critic who had questioned his mental ability because of his messy desk, Winston Churchill asked, "If a cluttered desk means a cluttered mind, what does an empty desk mean?" Way to go Winston!!
Remember, you can use organization as a way

s, but your success isn't
on your desk. It's your
ls, and how you take action.

**ful before. What makes
ow?"**: There are countless
people who found success after a long
period of dismal failures. Abraham Lincoln barely had a political resume (unless losing elections counts) before becoming the 16th president of the United States. Sally Jessy Raphaël was fired 18 times before she became the most popular daytime talk show host and earned millions of dollars.

- **"It takes money to make money"**: This is one of the most insidious beliefs that followed me from childhood. Sure, not having money is a legitimate obstacle. You can't start a business without money, even if you're operating on a shoestring budget. But does that mean you can't find money? Does it mean there's no way to *ever* start a new business? Here's the honest truth: it doesn't take money to make money – it takes a dream to make money. John Paul DeJoria and his partner Paul Mitchell invested $700 and founded the John Paul Mitchell Company that has made billions of dollars selling hair care products. In 1989 he formed The Patrón Spirits Company and in the process became a billionaire.

- **"My family/friends are bogging me down"**: The people around you do have a tremendous influence on your behavior and success. But if you let that be the sole variable that determines how much you achieve, you're always going to be limited by their opinions and not your opinion of yourself. Buying into how they see things can keep you from seeing the truth. So, do you want to keep indulging this limiting belief, or challenge it to see if it holds true? Do you want to stay bogged down in the life you have, or be living the life you want?

Of course, not all limiting beliefs are this obvious. Heck, you still might not be able to identify them after coming this far. So let's spend a little more time addressing limiting beliefs, and come up with a step-by-step way to identify and change them before they get a stranglehold on your dreams and goals.

A Guide to Changing Limiting Beliefs

Write down your dreams or goals

If you're reading this with the hopes of changing your limiting beliefs, odds are you have a dream or goal in mind. Even if it has yet to become a reality, this exercise can help you see it as a possibility.

There's less "mental clutter" to worry about when you organize your thoughts on paper. First, you don't have to expend energy having them bouncing around in your mind. And secondly, it improves your odds for success. Brian Tracy says your chances of reaching a goal are 1,000% greater if you've written it down. One thousand percent! That advantage is too big to ignore, so WRITE … IT … DOWN!

If you're not sure how to create a goal, you can get a free goals worksheet and training video at Get-Smart-Goals.com.

Write down why you feel you can't achieve your goal or dream

Think of this as a Rorschach test for your life. Write down what first comes to mind, no matter how bad it makes you feel. When you think about your goals, the thoughts that make you feel bad and helpless are likely the limiting beliefs you need to identify. Odds are that as they surface, you'll notice that some ring truer than others. **Circle these beliefs**, because they are the main limiting *assumptions* you're going to be addressing.

For each belief you circled, research examples of people who overcame that same limitation

If you think you're not attractive enough to land a leading role, think about A-list actors who don't fit the Hollywood mold of leading man (Steve Buscemi) or ingénue (Linda Hunt). If you think you're too short to play in the NBA, 5'9" Chicago Bulls Nate Robinson once blocked a lob by Houston Rockets 7'6" star, Yao Ming.

The more you research, the more you'll see that just about every hero you can think of had some limitation they had to overcome. Suddenly, it seems like the people *without* limitations are the ones at a disadvantage!

Re-write your beliefs in a positive way that allows you to take action

Now that you've researched real-world evidence to invalidate your negative beliefs, it's time to re-write your beliefs to fit the life you want.

For example, instead of "I <u>can't</u> start a successful business because I don't have a college degree," you should say "I <u>can</u> start a successful business without a college degree because it's been done many times by other people like ...., ... and ...."

Write this new belief on a piece of paper and post it where you'll see it on a regular basis. Read it out loud at least twice a day (first thing in the morning and last thing in the evening are great times), and you'll begin to feel a new, empowering belief changing your overall attitude and faith.

But this is just a taste of the power you can attain by simply changing your beliefs and your perceptions. So read on to learn more!

3

Metacognition, or How to Think About Thinking

By now you might have thought, *Hey, I'm a positive person. Why aren't I rolling in dough? Why isn't my business taking off? Why is there still a mound of bills on my desk? Why aren't I steamrolling toward success the way so many self-help gurus promised I'd be?*

Even though you may be familiar with the power of positive thinking, and may consider yourself one of the most positive people you know, the problem might be you haven't correctly developed how you think.

That brings us to the concept of metacognition – a fancy word describing the process of thinking about thinking. (In many ways this entire guide is an exercise in metacognition because it discusses the way you think.) You'll be amazed at how much you can discover about yourself if you gain an understanding of your own thought processes.

So let's start with an exercise that could represent the foundation for systematically changing your beliefs.

One Week of Thinking About Thinking

You did some recognition of limited beliefs in the previous chapter. But while that addressed some of your most powerful negative beliefs, you still have trapped misperceptions you didn't realize you were thinking.

Before you go on a crusade to change your thoughts, it's important to find any blind spots. (Would you ever consider changing lanes on a busy highway without checking for blind spots in your rearview mirror?) Identifying blind spots keeps your focus forward instead of constantly looking at what's behind you.

If this sounds ridiculous, give this exercise a try for a week and see how things add up. Starting tomorrow, carry a journal with you at all times as you're going to keep track of your thoughts. You don't have to document every thought, as it's hard to listen to the constant internal conversation you have running through your mind.

But if you catch yourself continually going back to the same thought, like how you're going to get all your bills paid, write it down. Your goal is to journal the thoughts you dwell on the most, and the ones you continually return to since they can do the most damage to you psychologically.

You'll have positive thoughts throughout a day such as congratulating yourself on a good morning of productivity. You'll also have neutral thoughts, like wondering what's on TV or what to make for dinner.

But what you might find disturbing about this exercise is that you have more negative thoughts than you realized. You might find yourself dwelling on some aspect you don't like such as your weight or lack of a college degree.

Many negative thoughts might seem trivial at the time, like thinking your nose is crooked. But thoughts are seeds, and given too much attention they can grow into much bigger things. And as the seeds grow, they sprout roots that can affect different areas of your thoughts and therefore your life.

People who have done this exercise have told me how lacking they were in the art of positive thinking. They didn't realize how often they were continually kicking themselves for one particular flaw or imagining a limited future.

Remember: Your belief doesn't have to be conscious for it to have a cataclysmic effect on your life. This experiment in metacognition might be uncomfortable, but it's the first crucial step in taking control of your thoughts and your life.

Will it be a pain in the neck to track your thoughts for a week? Probably, as mental work can be exhausting. Wallace Wattles, author of the classic *The Science of Getting Rich*, wrote "There is no labor from which most people shrink as they do from that of sustained and consecutive thought. It is the hardest work in the world." But it's also the most valuable work, as you'll soon learn.

I promise that the rewards of metacognition – of knowing your own thoughts – will help you. Otherwise, you'll be going through the motions of success and achievement with your blinders on. It would be like driving down a road at night with your lights off. Your journey will be much easier once you shine the light on the path ahead of you.

Turning Metacognition into Action

Once you have journaled a week of deep thoughts, you should notice some consistencies that paint an entirely new picture of what your thinking patterns look like. Even if the picture isn't pretty – which it most likely won't be because you're dealing with negative habits – there's one powerful realization you can reap from it: **You now have a road map for changing your thoughts**.

The Book of James says that 'faith without works is dead.' How true that is. Even armed with the weapon of metacognition, you still won't be able to change your results unless you do some fine-tuning on your thought processes.

That being said, there is one problem with all of the above: If you gear all of your work towards better beliefs at this point, you still won't be able to make real progress. You need action to support your efforts.

So how do you turn metacognition into action?

Study your journal carefully and try to recognize the thought patterns that strike you as being the most damaging (after you go through your notes a few times they should jump out at you). You don't have to find a specific *type* of pattern; just look at the thoughts that make you feel the weakest, saddest, and resonate with truth.

Go through each of those thoughts, and ask yourself if there's some way to put on the brakes before going down the path of habitual damaging behavior (i.e., having a big greasy dinner that makes you feel physically and emotionally bad about yourself).

Like in the chapter on overcoming limiting beliefs, your next step will be to nip those problems in the bud and turn them around. With this exercise you'll learn to stop your negative thinking even if it's with one small baby step. (You don't need to try to fix everything at once. Controlling one problem at a time will eventually end up in having overcome most of your negative thought processes.)

Let's say every time you check your bank account and see a low amount, you have thoughts of scarcity and desperation. The next time you check your bank account, decide that you're going to reinterpret your balance. Maybe you're living paycheck to paycheck, and your bank account could get as low as $25.

Instead of dwelling on how low that number is, think about it in a more positive light. Ask yourself what you could do with $25 for someone in need. You could take them to a nice lunch. Or you could buy and prepare a meal for their family. Or you could buy diapers for their new baby and so on.

Just like having to check your bank account from time to time, you can use that same sort of routine to start changing your thought processes.

A silly thought? Perhaps. But it interrupts the pattern of dwelling on what you don't have, and takes your thinking in a completely different direction. It takes a negative perception and turns it into a positive perception, no matter how insignificant it may seem at the time. On top of that, just the thought of doing something good for someone else will have a magical impact on your mental well-being.

I used to have a constant, nagging negative belief that I never had enough time. I always felt rushed or late getting out the door, everything had a deadline, I couldn't get things done on time. I was late… late… late! Every time I got in a bind for time, I immediately thought "I never have enough time!" and it would severely blacken my mood. This spilled into many areas of my life, and became an impediment to succeeding.

After I evaluated my *perception* of lack of time as a negative belief, I came up with a truth card (I'll be talking about those in a minute) that stated "**I always have enough time to do everything I need to do**." And that is the truth. I *don't* have time to do everything I *want* to do, but I *always* have time to do everything I need to do.

Establishing a habit of consciously thinking positively will eventually cause you to unconsciously think positively. What's important is that you focus on the good you want to accomplish or how you want to feel.

There are plenty of ways to change your thought patterns, and one is by planting seeds. And what feeds the seeds of your thoughts? *Paying attention*. By paying attention to new thoughts you're growing better thoughts. And heck, you might just notice other, better thoughts sprouting all around you.

Thoughts Snowball Too!

You'll notice that as you change your negative thoughts, something very peculiar – and even a bit miraculous – will start to happen. *Your new thoughts will have friends!*

Logically, changing yourself doesn't happen overnight. If you were to start training for a 5K marathon on Monday, you wouldn't be ready by Wednesday. Your new beliefs and attitudes will take time to fully settle in and become a regular part of your thought process.

But that doesn't mean you won't notice results right away. One of the easiest ways to see how thoughts change quickly is to notice how your new positive thoughts snowball. It might be hard to see at first, so let's look at an example.

You did the exercise in metacognition and decided to reshape a negative thought into something more positive to establish as a belief. Every day and night you'll think this thought in the form of an affirmation such as "Everywhere I turn I find new clients" (better yet say it out loud. When your ears hear it your mind believes it to be true.) You might feel a little silly doing the affirmation at first, as if you're convincing yourself of something that isn't true.

But then something happens.

Instead of focusing on how you wish you had more clients, you might feel resistance to your new belief because of something that's been missing in the real world. As you *resist* the new thought, your *focus* gives fuel to a new belief.

Suddenly a new thought springs up: "I forgot to buy advertising in my local paper last week!" Then you laugh when you realize, *How could I ever expect a new client to pop up if I'm not advertising my business?*

On the surface this affirmation scenario might seem like a failure. But if you hadn't affirmed your first thought – the *belief* you'd find a new client – you might have thought about something else instead of realizing you needed to buy advertising in order to get clients. By focusing on the goal, you start to shape tangible thoughts about the goal. The net results are that you have thoughts, ideas, and action items you wouldn't have had otherwise.

Keep on this course and your beliefs will start to snowball. One thought will lead to another to another and so forth. Not only will your first affirmations become easier, you will wonder how you ever doubted you could achieve your goal (such as landing new clients).

Dwell long enough on this new way of thinking, and the day will come when new clients (or whatever your needs are) will begin appearing – sometimes in the strangest of circumstances and places. As one of my mentors, Bob Proctor, said, "Thoughts become things. If you see it in your mind, you will hold it in your hand."

Thoughts don't exist in a vacuum. They permeate your actions, your beliefs, and even your faith, which is why even just one thought can snowball into something very profound. Heck, even *thinking* about your thoughts can be the stepping stone you've been waiting for.

That's why it's so important to journal your thoughts and see what kind of seeds you've been planting in your attitude and your beliefs. You are the gardener of your own mind and your own life. In the New Testament we are reminded that "...whatsoever a man soweth, that shall he also reap." (Galatians 6:7)

4

Four Ways to Introduce New Beliefs

After reading the previous chapters, you should have a better idea of what limiting beliefs and recurring thoughts are holding you back. Now it's time to replace old beliefs with new ones.

You'll likely never get to a place where all your thoughts are 100% positive. You'll never say, "Whew, I'm done! Thank goodness I got that whole belief thing handled," since experiences and events are constantly changing. What is important is to learn how to keep up with changing your negative thoughts into positive beliefs the minute you recognize them.

Growth in life is all about struggle and encountering resistance, and that *nothing* in life is static. Nothing stays unchanged. Even if your life appears to be at a standstill, it's not. You're either living or you're dying. There's nothing in between. To think otherwise would violate the known laws of the universe.

The following methods of introducing new beliefs will be fundamental to what you're trying to achieve. And what you can achieve in a short period of time just might astound you.

Method 1: Truth Cards

Some people use affirmations (mentioned above), but I use "truth cards." **Truth cards** are essentially reminders of the new *unlimiting* beliefs you want to hold. In using truth cards, you'll likely never go back to your old beliefs again.

In the chapter on overcoming limiting beliefs, I told you to write down replacement beliefs and place them where you could see them all the time. You can post your truth cards around your workspace as reminders of what you want to believe. You can carry them with you, and read them out loud as an affirmation of a new belief. (To this day my mentor, Bob Proctor, still carries his truth cards in his wallet to constantly remind him of his beliefs.)

Affirmations in any form are great tools. But there's something about the power of writing thoughts down on paper – or in this case, cards – that really solidifies a new thought as something you're going to work on. After all, the very act of writing something down is an affirmation in and of itself.

Always keep these truth cards with you. You'll not only be reminded of the new beliefs you want, but you'll eventually start to believe them. These cards need to become an inherent part of your life from now on, because the beliefs they contain will definitely shape your future.

During one of the worst financial times of my life, I came up with the idea for my truth cards because I didn't have extra money to do anything fancy. I found an old box of business cards I no longer used. I took a pen and drew a big X across the front of the card and flipped it over to the blank side where I wrote the truth about one of my negative beliefs. I picked up the next business card and did the same thing. I didn't quit until I had done more than 50 truth cards (that in itself was astounding – to realize that I had 50 beliefs I needed to restructure. Whew!)

I made two sets – one for my car and one for my office. Whenever I took a break, I would flip through the cards and read each one aloud, while adding as much emotion to the reading as I could muster (emotion is important as it makes you *feel* your affirmation). When I was in my car at a stop light, or waiting for someone to show up, I'd do the same (please *don't* read your cards while driving!).

Repeating this process thousands of times over several months had an incredible impact on my attitude, and gradually morphed the negative beliefs that were long embedded in my subconscious into positive behavior.

Some of my "truths" were passages I had read by Emmet Fox in his book *Make Your Life Worthwhile*. Some cards had biblical quotes reflecting my Christian beliefs. Some were quotes by authors that held a message of truth I wanted to embrace. As I progressed I began to produce my own new, meaningful truths I wanted to embrace in my life.

Here's an example of what some of my truth cards contained:

- I can do this and I know I can. (My number one card. I repeated this affirmation thousands of times during December 1997.)
- There is nothing or no situation you cannot overcome if you will believe.
- You cannot fully reach your potential until you have learned the principal of helping others reach theirs.
- A person is not limited by his environment. He creates his environment by his beliefs and feelings.
- All that's required is that you really believe and have no doubt. You can pray for anything, and if you believe you have it; it's yours. (Mark 11:23-24)

- You can change your thoughts and feelings, and then the outer things will change to correspond, and indeed there is no other way of working. (Emmet Fox)
- Quit thinking about all of the reasons why you can't do something, and think about all the reasons you can.
- If you have worthwhile goals and are going in the right direction, all your needs will be provided for (this one was critical for me to believe, because at the time I couldn't rub two nickels together most days).

For a FREE copy of my entire file of Truth Cards that you can personalize for yourself, go to GetMyTruthCards.com

I'm of the opinion that you can't use the truth cards too much. Most people won't get the results they're seeking, because they don't discipline themselves enough to affirm the "truths" until they take hold. If you act in faith that your truth cards will work – and you diligently, relentlessly work with them – you *will* feel your beliefs changing.

One of my cards was a quote from Napoleon Hill's *Think and Grow Rich*: "It is a well known fact that one comes, finally, to *believe* whatever one repeats to one's self, whether the statement be true or false." Nothing could state the importance of repetition more than that.

Method 2: Your Circle of Friends

If you hung out with Bill Gates or Donald Trump on a regular basis, do you think it would have an effect on your attitude? Do you think that what they knew would rub off on you?

Of course it would. After all, you're hanging out with billionaires. You'd probably get used to the idea that you can change the world, as Gates endeavors to do through the Bill & Melinda Gates Foundation. You couldn't *help* but change your beliefs because you'd be seeing real-world evidence of those beliefs in front of you.

Oprah Winfrey said, "Surround yourself with only people who are going to lift you higher." That's the power of your circle of friends, and it's a power you should never take lightly.

But there are two sides of this coin. First, you have to find people who already have the beliefs you want. Let's say you want to be a great chess player. You could get a lot of practice online. But how much better would your skills become if you hung out at chess meets and hobnobbed with some of the greatest players around?

One-on-one interactions have a far more potent effect on your beliefs. You'll begin to see that over-achievers might do extraordinary things, but they're just ordinary people. As this becomes firmly embedded in your subconscious, it will function as a huge boost to your belief. That's why clubs, outings, and networking events based around a single idea can be so great. You can meet people who are already in possession of the beliefs you're looking for.

Of course, making friends that way isn't always easy, as friendships sometimes have to develop organically. Wherever, whenever, however you make friends, make sure they have a positive effect on your attitude and not the opposite. You're working hard to build a positive foundation of your beliefs. Negative people can tear down your efforts so fast that your head will spin.

If you're at a loss as to where to find people you want to associate with, locate a Toastmasters chapter. (I guarantee that no matter where you live, there's one within driving distance. I've sent thousands of people to Toastmasters over the years). People have said to me, "Vic, why do I need to go to Toastmasters? I don't want to be a speaker." My answer is simple: "No matter what you do, at some point you're going to have to present your ideas to people, and Toastmasters helps you become a better presenter."

But the biggest reason to find a Toastmasters chapter is because *everyone* who goes to one of their meetings is seeking to improve themselves in some way. And they are the kind of people you want to be around. As the old saying goes, "a rising tide floats all boats." Being around a group of positive people who are working to improve themselves is going to have a profound impact on your belief system.

After you start hanging out with the right people, you need to *stop hanging out with people who bog you down.* (You know who they are. They're the ones who burst your bubble with their jealousy or anger about their own lives. Why would you want them around in the first place?)

If you truly want to *cultivate* a better attitude within yourself, you'll need to recognize the effects that people's negative beliefs have on your psyche. First and foremost, you have one shot at your life and you should live it as positively as possible.

Of course this won't be easy to do. Friendships can be hard to make, and many people would rather have depressing friends than no friends at all. You don't necessarily have to "fire" all your relationships; but you should adopt a "gardening" attitude to weeding out the thorns from your life. Eventually, and with consistent pruning, your garden will look lush and full of all the beauty you deserve.

So it is with your friendships. Start pursuing people that will be beautiful plants in your garden, and dig out the weeds. It might be hard at first, but in the long run you won't miss the negative effects you're cutting loose.

Method 3: Action

Huh? Now you're talking about action? Aren't beliefs just manifestations of thoughts? Can't you change your beliefs with mental instead of physical work? Vic, you're giving me a headache.

The more you continue with this program, the more you'll learn about the true connection between the mental and the physical. I mentioned earlier that you can't sit on your couch all day and expect an opportunity to come knocking at your door.

Why? It's because your actions are very similar to your thoughts.

Consider someone who trains relentlessly for a triathlon. They do a lot of mental preparation and visualization in order to be prepared for the big event. But training in the physical world is an *active* form of that preparation. It's *thought in motion*. Every day that triathlete goes to the gym, or swims, bikes and runs, they are *witnessing* a real-world affirmation of what they want to come true. They are taking it out of their mind into the physical reality of their body.

You think it's hard to change your abstract beliefs? Try believing that you're not ready for a triathlon after you've seen yourself take *action*! You won't be able to do it, because action is one of the most positive ways to reinforce new beliefs. You've had results, you've had proof that your belief has translated into something tangible.

- Taking action signals your subconscious that you're serious about your new beliefs.
- Taking action that you usually don't take helps you to see yourself in new roles and new identities.
- Taking action can be the shift in momentum you need for greater inspiration. You don't have to run a marathon. But if you run one mile today, you're more likely to run one or more tomorrow.

So don't ignore the role that action takes in providing the foundation for your new beliefs. There's no better way to convince yourself that a new reality is coming true than to go out and see it in person.

(In John 20:24, when St. Thomas doubted – the origins of a "doubting Thomas" – that Jesus had risen, Jesus appeared to him and said 'Have you believed because you have seen me? Blessed are those who have not seen and yet have come to believe.')

Also, remember that this doesn't need to be an either/or question. You don't have to choose between thinking yourself successful and acting yourself successful. If both your thoughts and actions align with a new goal and new belief, the success you achieve will astound you.

Method 4: Gratitude and Positive Emotions

I've stated before that thoughts don't exist in a vacuum, and this is all too true. Which is why you'll never really be able to dissociate thoughts from your emotions.

This isn't a bad thing, as thoughts can have either negative or positive emotions attached to them. You'll find, however, that thoughts associated with positive emotions can be incredibly powerful.

I've learned that gratitude is one of the most important emotions you can have to reinforce a belief. For example, think about the things you're sure about. If you're feeling *certain* about something or someone, you'll stay in a constant state of gratefulness.

Not everyone is blessed to have grown up with a great family, but let's say you were. If you see a friend suffering from family problems, and you think about your own family you were blessed with, what thought is going to come to your consciousness? You're going to be grateful for your own situation. You'll have an *unconscious affirmation* of your belief that you have a great family.

But you might say, "It's easy to be grateful when you already *have* what you want."

But that doesn't mean you can't be grateful, because you can be thankful for what you already have.

Did the sun rise this morning? Even though the

sun will provide light for many hours, it will go down at the end of a day. But right now it's lighting your day and allowing you to do whatever you want, so that's something to be grateful for.

Do you have enough money to keep from starving? That's worth being grateful for, because there are plenty of people in the world who don't have enough money to feed their family. Do you have enough clean water to drink? As stated earlier, this would be considered luxury to millions of people. Chances are you have plenty to be grateful for.

If you want to cultivate a feeling of gratitude, first ask yourself what you've been taking for granted. Then if you want to use gratitude to change your belief, you can do that too.

As Bob Proctor advocates, start an affirmation with "I'm happy and grateful now that..." "I am grateful that I've achieved a successful business," or "I am grateful that I've lost the weight I've been struggling with." Use gratitude as an emotion to connect yourself to something that has yet to appear in your life.

You can even be grateful for small things that occur throughout your day. "I am grateful that I ate that healthy salad instead of that fattening burger." Connecting beliefs to positive emotions will help you develop a good relationship with those beliefs.

In his 100-year-old classic, *How to Get What You Want,* Orison Swett Marden said, "People who take life sadly, who see nothing to rejoice and be glad about, not only lose a tremendous amount of pleasure and real enjoyment, but they seriously cripple their ability and impair their success. They are not normal, and therefore cannot reach their maximum of strength and efficiency."

If necessary, force yourself to feel grateful in the beginning. You'll find, like so many things in life, that change is simply a matter of making a decision. And once it becomes a habit, you'll experience peace like you never have before.

5

Changing Your Reality as a Result of Changing Your Belief

Perhaps the most mysterious thing about faith and belief are the direct results they have on people's outcomes. I'm not talking about how having a positive attitude about going to the gym will make you start going to the gym. I'm talking about an almost spooky level of results you can get when you change your belief.

Once you start accepting a new belief as true, you might notice:

- **Appearances of new opportunities**. Maybe you changed your belief in how much you can charge for a financial service you're offering. The next day a client comes in and, not knowing your prices offers that exact amount of money.

. Have you ever thought
n gotten a phone call from
unny, I was just thinking

ions. Let's say a co-worker
bout something. Once you
change your belief, you might notice that not only
do they stop nagging you, they disappear from
your life altogether (maybe they were transferred to
another division or quit the company).

Now, I'm not suggesting that you start believing in magic. But I am suggesting that your faith has a way of changing your circumstances in ways that you can't imagine. As they say, 'the universe works in mysterious ways.'

Ninety days after I started my personal campaign to eliminate my limiting beliefs, the right people and opportunities suddenly appeared. I never understood how all of that happened – I just knew it did. And I knew the change came *after* I changed my beliefs.

I like to use the analogy that I've never understood how electricity works, but it doesn't stop me from walking over to a wall and flipping on a light switch. Faith and belief are your keys for flipping on some pretty unbelievable switches in your life!

Conscious/Unconscious Attention: A Major Mechanism for Success

Sometimes referred to as the "reticular activating system," your brain's vehicle for bringing things to your conscious attention can be manipulated to help you sniff out opportunities before the other guys.

In short, that which you think about the most will most frequently come to your attention.

The classic method of testing this theory is to have students close their eyes, and tell them they're going to notice everything in the room that is the color green. Then they will open their eyes and have ten seconds to find everything green.

Then the students will close their eyes again, and will be asked to tell you everything they saw in the room that was *red*. Most of them will have no idea as they were only looking for the color green. Even if there were plenty of objects that were red, the students might have *seen* them but they certainly didn't *notice* them.

Here's a profound concept: The reticular activating system doesn't just work with colors.

For those years when I was broke, I dreamt of owning a Cadillac Escalade. At the time it seemed to be the king of all vehicles. Several times a month, I would stop by the local Cadillac lot after they had closed, and peeked inside all the shiny new Escalades sitting on the lot, dreaming about the day I would own one.

I really had a desire for an Escalade, and certainly part of that desire was that it's an exclusive vehicle. Because of the high price most people can't afford one, so I suppose that "exclusivity" appealed to me.

In December 2004, just two days before Christmas, I went down to the Cadillac lot that I had been cruising. Only this time I went there to bring home my dream vehicle with its special "White Diamond" tri-coat paint job, and it was exciting!

Now, imagine my surprise when just a few days later it seemed that everywhere I looked I saw White Diamond Escalades. I'd pull up to a light and there'd be one next to me and on the other side of the street. Now that I owned one, it seemed like a lot of other people did as well. I had the depressing thought that my long-awaited dream machine was just as common as an everyday Toyota.

But I didn't realize that I was seeing the *results* of my *reticular activating system*, the unconscious part of the brain that recognizes thoughts and reorganizes the world to better suit those thoughts. It's just trying to do you a favor by helping to make things happen.

This is a powerful epiphany, because the ability to see what had previously been blind spots can be magical. It can have a profound effect on your success, and bring opportunities to your attention that seem to appear out of nowhere.

The beauty of your mind bringing things to your attention is that you simply have to think about something over and over. Again, focus is to thoughts as what water is to plants. With focus, your thoughts will grow and blossom. Without focus, they will wither and die.

Combining Faith with Action

While blind *faith* can be a good thing (sometimes you have to set a goal well before you can see it appear in reality), blind *action* can lead to a lot of frustration. Taking action toward a goal can be a great momentum builder. Taking a first step – no matter how arbitrary it may be – of course is vitally important. But you shouldn't be taking action just for the sake of taking action.

So how do you prevent that? You have to *combine faith with action.*

Let's say you want to build a new house. Would you start chopping down trees and digging a hole? Or would the first step you take combine faith and action through *active planning*? If you've ever built a home, you know you first need blueprints and then start building from the ground up. Similarly, you can't build a skyscraper until you've designed the blueprints and have dug a very deep foundation.

That's why the more planned your action is – and the

more you have a *clear picture* of what you want to achieve – the more you'll be able to see yourself achieving that goal.

A great way to ground your action with faith is to develop concrete plans for your goals. If you want to lose weight, develop a workout plan. If you have a business, start a to-do list for long-term tasks. Keep your plans visible so you know what the next step is. The more visual evidence of your progress you begin to notice, the better.

Taking action will change your life, but it will be all the more potent if you can combine faith with action. Faith isn't just *believing* that you'll get to your goal; it starts with *seeing* the ending from the very beginning.

Remember Paul the apostle's wisdom we covered earlier: "Faith is the substance of things hoped for, the evidence of things not seen." Seeing the end from the very beginning is both the substance of things hoped for, and the evidence of things not seen. This is **very powerful** (you might want to write this on one of your truth cards).

Think about it like a puzzle. At the beginning you start with a picture on the box that represents what you'll be putting together. You just have all of the pieces, but don't see the completed puzzle.

You have a plan in place (the picture), and you start working. You connect two pieces, then two more and two more, and so on. The more connections you make, not only will your faith that you'll finish the puzzle increase, but you'll have more of the overall goal achieved as you start to see the picture come together.

Combine all your thoughts (the puzzle pieces) into a single effort (the finished picture), and you're bound to be successful.

Opportunity from Thought

In one of the previous sections, I mentioned how your focus literally determines what you're capable of noticing in your environment. Think about green, and you're likely to see more green. It's not that there are suddenly more green things around you; you're just noticing them more. Let's take that concept a step further, because there's more here than meets the eye.

Using this internal mechanism for focus and attention can help you recognize new opportunities. But even if you're making a conscious effort to notice new things, what if your sights are too low? What if your aim could be higher?

Building exciting new opportunities as a result of your belief doesn't mean you should look only for opportunities that *fit* your situation. You should use your focus to *change* your situation. And that means setting your sights higher.

Let's say you own a consulting business that only brings in $20,000 gross. You've worked as hard as you can.

So you know that if you're going to make more money, you're going to have to charge more for your services.

The problem? You have the belief that your services are only worth the $50 per hour you've been charging. In order to convince other people that your services are worth $200 per hour, you're going to have to bring yourself out of the $50 per hour mindset.

If you took the previous section on the reticular activating system to heart, you can start focusing on providing $200 per hour services, even if you're not sure how to get there.

What happens next is perhaps the most important step of the process, because it's where you will either accept or reject new possibilities. You'll encounter resistance similar to bench pressing weights for the first time.

As you start to think in terms of $200/hour, you'll be faced with your limiting beliefs: *I don't think my services are worth that much. More experienced consultants have better clients. My clients can't afford me at this rate. No one will want to work with me if I charge that much. It's an outrageous amount.*

Being a persistent believer, you decide to use the chapter on limiting beliefs to your advantage. You take those opposing statements and print them out on truth cards. While you may not fully believe them as yet, at least you can see the words: "My services are worth $200 per hour." "I have clients that can easily afford me at this rate." "Everyone wants to work with me at $200 per hour." "$200 is a reasonable amount because I always give more in value than I charge." Once you commit to making *these* beliefs your new attitude, you've made the first major shift in your thinking.

So what's likely to follow? You'll start having other thoughts – just little sprinkles at first – that support your new assertions. *There are companies out there that can afford $200 or more per hour. I just need to find them.*

Suddenly, you're on the path to changing your entire attitude and strategy. Eventually, you'll start noticing the $200 per hour opportunities you hadn't noticed before. Of course you could have chosen to change your beliefs to notice more $50/hour opportunities, but you'd be selling yourself short. Once you sign that first contract for $200 per hour, you'll start to wonder what other possibilities might be waiting for you.

A colleague and I were speaking at a seminar about our mutual experiences with the incredible book, *The Magic of Thinking Big*, by Dr. David Schwartz. My friend had flown to Australia to pitch a prospective client he had sized up as being a $50,000 client. He had packed the book as it had been some time since he had read it. Although he had read it more than a dozen times, he thought it was a good opportunity to refresh his memory.

Just before going to bed he read Dr. Schwartz's book for about 25 minutes. He got up the next morning thinking he might be wrong asking for higher fees if his proposal was accepted.

He forged ahead and presented the proposal he had originally created, but had upped the price from $50,000 to $250,000. Even more amazingly he was *expecting* the client to accept it, which he did when he accepted the proposal at a cool quarter of a million dollars!

That 25-minute period of reading Dr. Schwartz's book changed the belief my friend had about the value of his services by a factor of five. And by acting on that belief he realized the manifestation of his belief!

6

Leaving The Old You Behind

Have you ever been out in the woods, only to be startled by something that looked like a snake? Upon closer inspection you realized it wasn't a live snake, but the skin it had shed.

In order to grow, snakes have to shed their skin. In order to fly, butterflies first have to form a chrysalis to protect the pupa. When they are fully grown they emerge and leave their old bodies behind.

Similarly, changing your beliefs can be scary because it will feel like you're leaving a bit of your old self behind. (If you follow my advice on spending less time with friends who bog you down, it can really feel like that. You are leaving behind the parts of your life that no longer work to embrace the new parts that do.)

The fear of the unknown is part of the resistance you'll

encounter along the way, but it's necessary to becoming a new person. The question you'll have to ask yourself is, is it worth it? Almost 100% of the time the answer is a resounding **Yes!**

Staffing Your Weakness

Many people have fears about their weaknesses, and don't believe they can achieve their goals because of their limitations. For example, let's say you're bad with numbers. You wonder how can you run a successful business if you're bad with numbers?

The solution is to do what's called "staffing your weakness." (You probably do some form of that now.) Maybe you don't cut your own hair because you know someone else can do it better. Or maybe you don't cook your own steaks because you know a restaurant that has aged meat and can cook it better.

Hiring or partnering with people to cover for your weaknesses is not just a sly way to get by in the world of business, it's a way of the world. And it's a strategy that should smash any remaining limiting beliefs you might have about yourself.

If you don't have enough money to hire employees, there are countless businesses or freelancers there that can do a great job on an as-needed basis. Heck, they're probably clamoring to work for you in this tight economy. No matter what your weakness is – be it marketing, accounting, writing, personal nutrition, etc. – you can replace that weakness with the talent and expertise of others.

You can give up your limiting belief about whatever talent you feel you lack as there is someone who can **staff your weakness**. If you're great at coming up with ideas, but you can't seem to get past the drawing table, you need an implementer. And there are implementers looking for people who have great ideas.

The key here is to know one simple fact: *That you are the one in control.* You can choose to take control of your success by taking proactive steps to staff your weaknesses. Or you can choose to indulge your weaknesses and never take any action to support your efforts. Believing you're not in control will be reflected in your real-world outcomes. You'll have to cover your own weaknesses, and will feel out of control as a result.

Some of the world's greatest leaders knew that they weren't everything to everybody. Henry Ford couldn't run every step of the assembly line to make his automobiles, so he hired people to do that for him.

Smart people know that working with even smarter people is the best decision you can make. Not only will it create better results for you in the long run, but will help you avoid any problems if you try to take care of everything yourself.

Even if you have to start hiring your weaknesses one step at a time – say, a business consultant or a virtual assistant for a few hours – you'll see how this process can eliminate limiting beliefs, and show you what you can really accomplish with the help of others.

The *old* you might have tried to overcompensate for weaknesses. The *new* you knows that working with people who are strong in the areas you aren't can help you overcome just about any limiting belief there is. Now you just need to leave that old you behind.

New Standards, New Challenges

Remember the previous example of jumping from $50 to $200 per hour? You might have read that and said "Sheesh, Vic, for $200 an hour I'd have to provide an insanely high standard for quality of work." If you felt reluctance about meeting this new standard, it's likely the result of a limiting belief you have.

True, raising your standards for success does mean encountering new challenges. But it's a limiting belief to assume those challenges will overwhelm you. Don't forget that your mind is wired to adjust to new standards. When you first drove a car with a driver's ed teacher, did accelerating from street to highway driving feel like a potential disaster? How does it feel now that you've had years of experience under your belt? You probably think of merging onto a highway a normal part of a daily commute.

Your new life doesn't have to become harder as the result of success. Leaving the old you behind means embracing a stronger you capable of meeting challenges head on and with less difficulty. Heck, isn't everyone after an easier life?

Once you've adjusted to a higher standard, you'll likely wonder how you ever allowed yourself to work for a lower standard before. But if you're still not convinced, here are a few strategies for dealing with the higher amounts of money, strength, and success that come as a result of more affirmed beliefs:

- **Keep your life simple**. Once people find some financial success, they start signing up for a bunch of subscriptions, TV channels, car loans, etc. You don't have to have all of these things just to prove you're successful; you can keep your life as simple and easy to manage as you'd like.

- **Add more weight**. Getting stronger in the gym means that everything will become less challenging as you bulk up. And it's your responsibility to keep that challenge up if you want to continue to grow. Add more weight to that "bench press" by raising the consulting rates at your business. Push yourself harder in everything you do. One significant challenge in achieving a new standard is avoiding the temptation to rest on your laurels.

- **Staff your weakness.** We dealt with this in the previous section, but it bears repeating: If there's ever an aspect of your life or your business you can't manage, all that's required of you is to find someone who can manage it for you.

Your fears that the challenges of future success will be too great are completely unfounded. After all, ask yourself how challenging it is to be poor and in ill health, and you'll know in which direction you should go.

Asking "What If?" and "How?" Questions

Leaving your old self behind won't be easy, no matter how much you want to do it, as your thought patterns and habits are well-engrained in your subconscious. It can be difficult to believe a truth card or affirmation when deep down you still feel as if the new assertion doesn't ring true. Therefore, asking "what if?" and "how?' questions can help you overcome this challenge.

For example, let's say this affirmation is too much for you to swallow: "I am so happy and grateful now that I earn $250,000 in a year." If the most you've ever earned in a year is $65,000, you'll feel like that affirmation is way out of your league.

So let's reposition this affirmation to "**What if** I earned $250,000 this year?" Suddenly, the thought isn't so challenging as it's now a possibility, it's something to ponder. You'll start thinking of all the fun things you could do if you had that money. You'll imagine all the toys you could buy, the place you might move to, or the debts you could pay off. By planting a seed of a positive thought – a seed of possibilities – you've found a way to think even more positive thoughts, and it didn't even require a difficult affirmation.

Now, you can get even more proactive with that affirmation by asking the "how" question: "**How** could I earn $250,000 in a year?" Suddenly the thought has gone from a daydream to an action plan. Saying "I *can't* earn $250,000 in a year" is a limiting belief that could make you want to quit before you try. But asking the "how" question demands a positive answer and a result. It forces you to think of possibilities because the "what if" made something tangible.

You'll probably have to tackle some of your limiting beliefs. "I'm stuck in my job; they won't triple my salary" isn't an answer to the $250,000 question. A real answer to the "how" would be something like "I'd have to raise my prices or find new customers." Or "I need to find a better-paying job. But I'd have to keep earning money at my current job in the meantime."

Suddenly you're thinking about actual **action steps** that can propel you toward your goal. And all because you took the edge off of the affirmation and asked yourself "what if" and "how" questions.

I clearly remember the process I went through when I wanted to earn $1,000,000 for the first time. It seemed so far out of reach and such a foreign concept, but I persisted with the "how" questions. I first thought that I could get one million customers at one dollar each, but one million new customers seemed unfathomable.

Then I thought I could get 100,000 customers at $10 each, but the 100,000 still seemed like a really large number. But I continued on with 10,000 customers at $100 each, 1,000 customers at $1,000 each and so on. Now these were numbers I could get my head around. I knew it would be a challenge, but I could literally "see" 1,000 customers. All I needed was to find 100 customers a month for ten months, and I knew I could create something of value at $1,000.

This whole process created a feeling of incredible energy and action because my faith was strengthening my belief. As it turned out, it ended up being closer to 4,000 customers at an average of $250. And now when I look back, it all seems so simple that I can't imagine why it took me so long to make $1,000,000.

If you remember how important the role of momentum is in changing your beliefs, you'll realize how life changing these empowering questions can be.

Letting Go of the Past

"The past is prologue to now" means people use their past as a springboard into a better and brighter future.

That's a noble concept. But I'd like to take it one step further: "All you need to know about your past is that it's created your current circumstances." Other than the lessons you've learned, there's not much you can do about it as the past has come and gone. You simply have to use the present to create a much better future, and you won't get very far if you're stuck in one place.

After all, the past is where some of your most negative limiting beliefs reside. It's where you learned to think "I can't do this because I never have." Or "I can't do this because I tried it once and failed."

Forget all that and instead ask yourself a "what if" question. "What if life could really change if I could change my beliefs? What kinds of beliefs would I change?"

Exercises like the metacognition steps help you monitor your thoughts in the present (which is why it's important to realize that a negative past can't help you find your way to the future unless you choose to view it in another way).

Remember the example of the twins who had different outcomes they attributed to the very same reason from their past (their alcoholic parents)? You need to learn how to view your negative thoughts in a completely different way to turn them into positive thoughts to get you where you want to go.

The past contains perceptions of your entire life's history. You can change (and even eliminate) those perceptions when you're ready to tear down the monuments you've built to your failures.

It's time to start creating a better future, and the choice is yours to make.

conclusion

As You Think, So You Are

In James Allen's landmark work of self-help, *As a Man Thinketh*, he wrote that the way you think is not just how you perceive things. Ultimately, it's how you create the experiences in your life.

But the truth is, most things do begin with perception. And the good news is changing your perceptions is easier than you think.

Bob Proctor uses a great "visual" example about changing perceptions. He asks you to drop your problem or circumstance into the middle of a big circle. Wherever you're standing, you're viewing your circumstance from a particular point of view.

But what happens if you walk along the circle until you're standing on the other side directly opposite from where you started? Now looking at your circumstance from a totally different viewpoint will change your perception as you're looking at it from a completely different angle. The circumstance didn't change – your perception did.

I use this example when speaking to an audience: "Imagine that on your way home today from this event you have a flat tire. Would that be a negative circumstance for you?" The audience nods their heads.

"Would that be a negative circumstance for the tow truck driver? Of course not, because your breakdown means income for him. So how can it be a negative circumstance for you and a positive circumstance for the tow truck driver? Easy. Circumstances are never positive or negative – they are always neutral. It's only your perception that makes it positive or negative. It depends what side you're looking at it from."

After waiting a moment for it to sink in, I continue: "Now, while the tow truck driver is replacing your tire, he notices a problem with your brakes that could cost you hundreds of dollars if left uncorrected. His observation just saved you a bunch of money. Do you still feel negative about your circumstance?"

Of course the audience shakes their heads, because they now have a different perspective of the situation. Every circumstance in your life has the same beginning. It is always a neutral event waiting for you to decide whether it will become positive or negative.

Reading this book can cause two emotions: First, **elation**. It's great news to learn that you're in charge of your own reality. And that you can begin changing it this very moment is a tremendously exciting and joyful epiphany. You'll always want to carry it with you, because it will help you to avoid the victim mindset and focus instead on proactive measures you can take to change your life.

But you might also experience **trepidation**. After all, the prospect that you're in charge of what you experience can be a daunting notion. You've been taught your entire life that you are the result of environment, nature, nurture (or lack thereof) and circumstances – anything but your own thoughts and beliefs.

How do you start thinking yourself into a better reality if all you encounter is resistance to your beliefs? If you're still confused about where to go from here, let me offer a little advice: take baby steps of action. Thought alone can get you to a certain point. But without action, you're not utilizing all the tools at your disposal. Action, after all, is simply another form of thought.

So which baby step should you take? It can start with something as simple as a to-do list on a yellow legal pad. Just make sure that you're taking consistent action from this point forward, because you'll never regret tomorrow if you take positive action today.

You only get one chance at this thing called life, so it's important not to waste any time indulging your most negative and draining beliefs. And you certainly don't want to waste it when you know you can change, and are being too fearful or self-doubting to make the journey.

Can you remember times when you felt hesitant about your own abilities, but once you started everything turned out okay? It might have been when you had to deliver a speech and were so nervous that you could feel your palms sweat. Yet afterwards you were excited and elated at what you'd accomplished. Or when you go to the gym your muscles are stiff and you don't feel like exercising, but you later emerge feeling like you can accomplish anything. Like learning to ride a bicycle for the first time, once you've mastered an ability you will feel victorious!

That law of momentum can work for and against you, so you need to push against the resistance and you'll come out stronger on the other end.

Don't ever – *ever* – sell yourself short. Expand your mental scenarios for success. Why are so many people to achieve wealth and happiness? Is there some magic quality like handsomeness or intelligence they have that you don't? Heck no! You just need to believe in yourself, and you'll be able to accomplish anything you put your mind to.

That, my friend, is the power of faith and a well-placed belief. First, it will change the way you view your world, and then it will change your world.

The title of this book wasn't chosen because it was catchy or cutesy. It was chosen because it's an undeniable truth: ***Believe in Yourself, and The Universe Will Be Forced to Believe in You!***

All you need to do is find what your beliefs are and take action!

Thank you for joining me on this journey to helping you find the success you deserve.

For a free book of
Napoleon Hill's classic
***Think and Grow Rich,* go to:**
www.Get-My-Free-Book.net.

URGENT PLEA!

Thank you for purchasing my master's book! It will really help life around here. Would you please help Vic (and me) and go back to the site where you purchased this book and leave your feedback. He needs your feedback to make the next version better. Arf! Arf!

Other Books from Laurenzana Press

The Strangest Secret by Earl Nightingale

Memory Improvement : How to Improve Your Memory in Just 30 Days by Ron White

Persistence & Perseverance: Dance Until It Rains by The Champions Club

The Law of Attraction: How To Get What You Want by Robert Collier

Time Management Tips: 101 Best Ways to Manage Your Time by Lucas McCain

Get Motivated: 101 Best Ways to Get Started, Keep Going and Finish Strong by Lucas McCain

Successful & Healthy Aging: 101 Best Ways to Feel Younger & Live Longer by Lisa J. Johnson

Self Confidence Secrets: How To Be Outgoing and Overcome Shyness by Lucas McCain

Happiness Habits: 21 Secrets to Living a Fun and Outrageously Rewarding Life by Lucas McCain

Self Help Books: The 101 Best Personal Development Classics by Vic Johnson

Overcoming Fear: 101 Best Ways to Overcome Fear and Anxiety and Take Control of Your Life Today! by Lucas McCain

Public Speaking Fear? 21 Secrets To Succeed In Front of Any Crowd by Lucas McCain

Going Green : 101 Ways To Save A Buck While You Save The Earth by Lucas McCain

Stress Management : 101 Best Ways to Relieve Stress and Really Live Life by Lucas McCain

Should I Divorce? 11 Questions To Answer Before You Decide to Stay or Go by Jennifer Jessica

Divorce Recovery: 101 Best Ways To Cope, Heal And Create A Fabulous Life After a Divorce by Lisa J. Johnson

Should I Have a Baby? 10 Questions to Answer BEFORE You Get Pregnant by Jennifer Jessica

Stop Procrastinating: 101 Best Ways to Overcome Procrastination NOW! by Lucas McCain

Think and Grow Rich : The Lost Secret by Vic Johnson

Should I Get Married ? 10 Questions to Answer Before You Say I Do by Jennifer Jessica

Meditation Techniques: How To Meditate For Beginners And Beyond by Lucas McCain

Fast NLP Training: Persuasion Techniques To Easily Get What You Want by Lucas McCain

How To Attract a Woman: The Secret Handbook of What Women Want in a Man by Jennifer Jessica

Cure Anxiety Now! 21 Ways To Instantly Relieve Anxiety & Stop Panic Attacks by Lucas McCain

About The Author

Eleven years ago Vic Johnson was totally unknown in the personal development field. Since that time he's created six of the most popular personal development sites on the Internet. One of them, AsAManthinketh.net has given away over 400,000 copies of James Allen's classic book. Three of them are listed in the top 5% of websites in the world (English language).

This success has come despite the fact that he and his family were evicted from their home sixteen years ago and the next year his last automobile was repossessed. His story of redemption and victory has inspired thousands around the world as he has taught the powerful principles that created incredible wealth in his life and many others.

Today he serves more than 300,000 subscribers from virtually every country in the world. He's become an internationally known expert in goal achieving and hosted his own TV show, Goals 2 Go, on TSTN. His book, *13 Secrets of World Class Achievers,* is the number one goal setting book at both the Kindle store and Apple iBookstore. Another best seller, *Day by Day with James Allen,* has sold more than 75,000 copies and has been translated into Japanese, Czech, Slovak and Farsi.

His three-day weekend seminar event, Claim Your Power Now, has attracted such icons as Bob Proctor, Jim Rohn, Denis Waitley and many others.

His websites include:

AsAManThinketh.net

Goals2Go.com

MyDailyInsights.com

VicJohnson.com

mp3Motivators.com

ClaimYourPowerNow.com

GettingRichWitheBooks.com

LaurenzanaPress.com

Made in the USA
Middletown, DE
25 September 2015